Bedding Plants For My Father

Alex Barr

Cover design based on an image
sourced from pixabay.com

ISBN: 9798361282975

Cerasus Poetry

London N22 6LY

cerasuspoetry.com

Dedicated to my ancestors and descendants, with love.

Contents

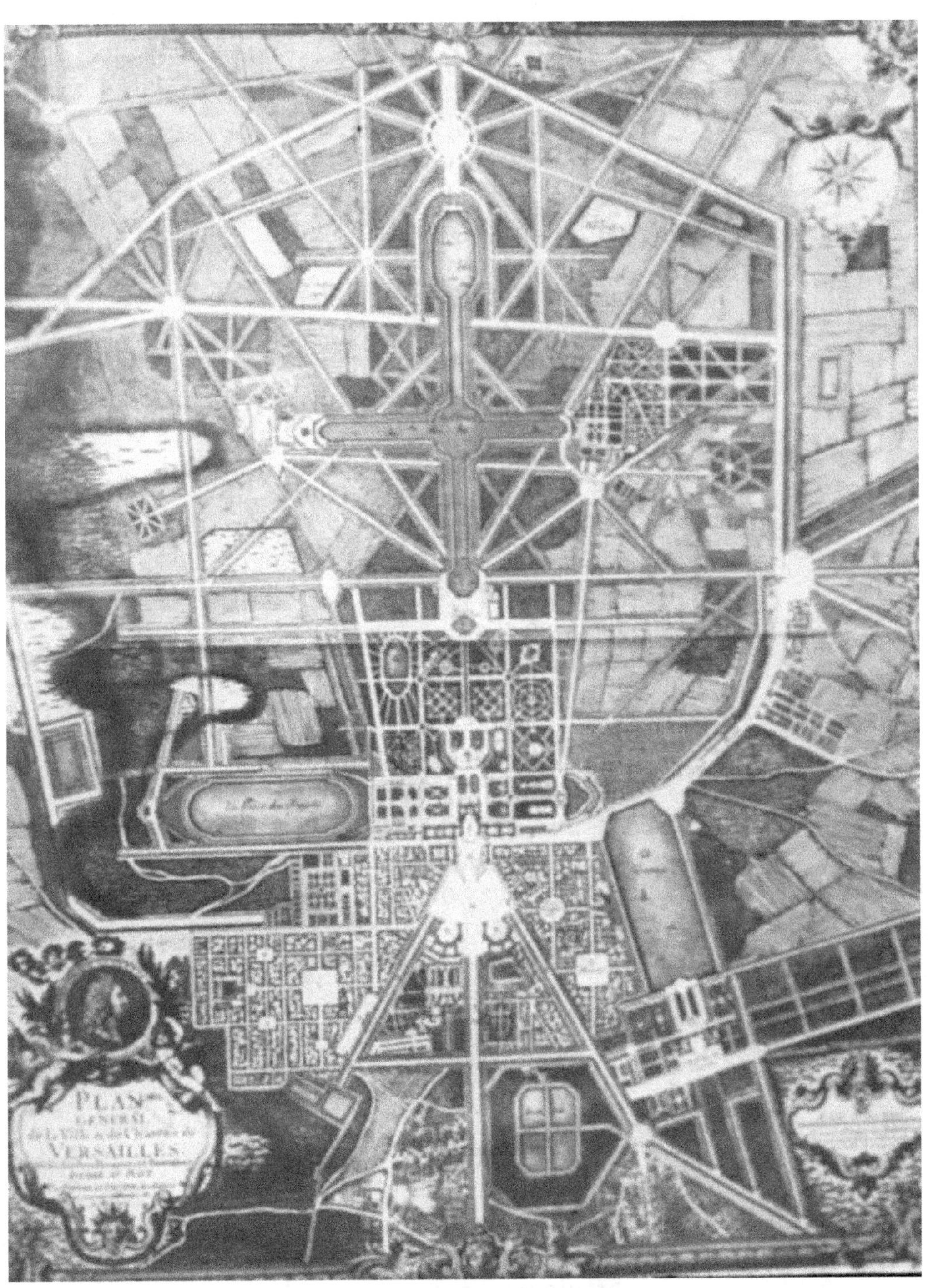
PLAN
VERSAILLES

Passion

(for my Great Uncle Charlie)

I pitied your stoop, stick,
  air of a wasted Churchill,
your talent (all artistic),
  your tale (commercial).
Your life studies were violets
  and ladies' heads,
your living selling sheets
  for well-feathered beds.

I pitied your marriage: Flo
  (whose clothes were made
by Liberty, London, no
  expense too great),
a month after you wed
  declared she did not
like ladies' heads,
  burned the lot.

I pitied your death in mean
  back-street quarters,
cash, ambition gone,
  no son, no daughter:
you who once bore samples
  on chauffeured wheels
and spatted feet to Maples,
  Harrods, Heals.

But once (do you remember?)
  you held our family
with Tennyson's *Defence*
  of Lucknow, from memory
– over a hundred lines.
  That was an occasion!
Victorian *politesse*
  threatened by passion.

Great Uncle's *Golden Treasury*

Here in the book you bought
And signed a century ago
Some of the pages are still uncut.
I'll slice them now.
Here's Rossetti's 'Sudden Light':

I have been here before,
But when or how I cannot tell:
I know the grass beyond the door,
The sweet keen smell . . .
Lines that in fifty years you never saw.

Oh armchairs. Oh collar – stiff.
Oh voice – reedy, refined, and wary.
Oh Great-Aunt's corsets creaking if
Life was too literary.
Oh oil of macassar massacring your quiff.

Dark Iron

(for my paternal grandfather)

Late in life, Granddad
I'm trying to use your plane
a dense baulk of timber
seventeen inches long.

Punched into it
are two short names:
yours on the flat front,
your father's in the throat
from days I can't imagine.

I'm using it badly.
It pitches. It wallows.
Judders along this door edge like
a launch in a thumping sea.
Floods of rough pine
fill the mouth.

I curse. I kick.
Your granddaughter-in-law
comes to see what sullies
the fine spring air.
'How do I set,' I fume,
'this bastard of a blade?'

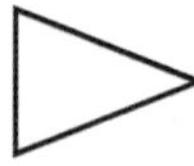

She fingers the superstructure
the high arabesque of handle
the dark iron before it
burred by blows
remembers her woodwork lessons:
'Tap the wooden wedge
then the blade – calmly.'

Tapping slowly
in small adjustments I
lose myself. Soon
through the throat
pour silver waves of shavings.

The door edge is level
a long shining loch
your plane travels over
in racing trim.

Your name on the nose
is my name.

A Haiku

For my maternal grandfather

Granddad Jim when hit
did what Christians rarely do:
turned the other cheek.

Half Moon Ride

(for my mother)

Two twenty-seven, light rain falling, a little heat
from the hedge banks. A hard slow pedal uphill
to mail your card. A charming finger-post
from the days when you were a girl
tempts me with black iron letters on white wood
to Crockernwell . . . but mine has to be the road
across the bridge (a stone one you'd approve of)
and the brown racing river.

By the black pump that reigns
over the village square I post
the damp card with its bland words, then freewheel
back to the snug half-hidden house
with the Flash and Sifta salt
and someone saying, 'We've got an hour, it's four.'

Always at four
you put away the brush and Brasso and went
upstairs. I waited for your transformation
from Mrs Mopp into a movie star.
Down you came down in a cloud of eau-de-cologne
with a painted Mona Lisa mouth
and drank tea from a cup
with a scalloped rim, because in those days
mugs were enamel, for bus-drivers and soldiers.

Your card will have left its red box by now.
I should have written Thank You
for those cosy afternoons with rain outside
(the radio playing the overture from Carmen,
or 'Enjoy Yourself, It's Later Than You Think')
and thanked you for much more, on a long roll of card
posted like a prayer-wheel before you die.

You'd like this room, the rain
diving off the eaves, the tabby asleep on cushions.
Enjoy yourself.

Daffodil Ride

Today is your first birthday in heaven.
On earth you would be ninety. This afternoon I rode
from Middle Mill to Whitchurch – hard, uphill
– then passed the abandoned airfield, empty
of the Eisteddfod, empty of lovely August.
The sky was colourless, and nothing moved until
innumerable starlings like a wave
swirled and shimmered down to sanctify
the sad fields with life.

At the Cathedral, passing the Deanery,
I remembered how I pushed your wheelchair
up the steep tarmac path. The precious weight of you
not to be spilled. Spilled now. And the daffodils were out
on the lawn of Bwthyn-y-Twr. And I lit a candle
and another man lit a candle
(but neither asked who the other was lighting for)
and we carried them south passing the shrine
of Dewi Sant into the other transept
(the one you and I once lit candles in)
and the other man placed his on
the middle tier of the black rack. Not wishing
to elevate or downgrade you I placed yours
on the same tier as his.

And there was a book in which one asked for prayers
for those in pain or trouble. *My friend is dying
of cancer*, was one. *He will leave two young boys.
Pray for him.* So I prayed. And realising you are so filled with love
you have no need of prayer, I left, and rode away.

Another Haiku

At your funeral
Reverend read your CV
for a job in heaven.

Bedding Plants For My Father

The daily *vierge* the Sun King deflowered
wasn't an individual to him
but pattern-fodder, like these ageratums
Mother says must be formal.

My heart resists. My heart is Japanese,
prefers the brush-stroke to the ruler's line.
Symmetry is a graveyard.

'We're doing it for your Dad,' she says. I see him
up in the cloud rack squinting past his thumb:
Blue, five inches, blue, five inches, white.

The little plants aren't eager to conform,
their stems not centred on their root balls.
I heave one half an inch sideways in the soil.

Mother says Dad loved these ritual rows
because my Granddad worked for the Duke of H –
whose gardener was his friend and taught him order.

And suddenly I remember how the Duke
had called his country home Chatellherault
and must have gardened in the French tradition.

Blue, five inches, blue, five inches, white.
This is Versailles, this is the Sun King's bed.

Waiting For You To Come Home

(for my wife)

Remember the first time
I opened my door to you?
Long before that, when

the Great Bear was over the wood
when I trod the seaweed
on Llanfairfechan beach

when Martin showed me
a snapped-off blade grown deep
in the furrows of an oak

when I sang in the gang-show
These are the times
you will dream about

you existed somewhere
and though I imagined you
I never imagined *You.*

A moment ago I noticed
blue and yellow ribs of sky
framed in a window feathered

with flying seeds caught on cobwebs.
And now? Another moment
moored in silence

a rusty honey extractor
a loaf without an end
a handful of dates.

Dark Matter

'I don't *know*,' I murmured
among drying terry nappies
in the Crouch End flat
where Kennedy was murdered,
when you asked unhappily
after we put the light out,
'Do you love me?'

'I don't know what love *is*,'
I answered and felt
the space between us empty.
I would have told you more
last night as you settled
to sleep, your crinkled eyelids
closed, the familiar angle of black lashes,
the cover hiding your cheek
under its blue stars. But shyness,
not wanting to wake you, held me back.

Today at dusk
you drove to a meeting saying,
'Back for dinner before I go out again.'
A month ago we still enjoyed
pink-and-gold sunsets at seven.
Now the sky disappears at six.
Where are you? Not hungry?
The pasta is sludge, the boiling water lava.
Your voice would calm the thud of the clock.

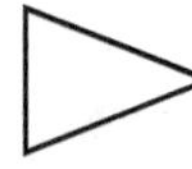

On TV news there are floods,
a malign glimmer of lakes.
A girl cries, her precious books awash,
and I rush without a torch into
the greedy lampless murk.
No flourish of headlights where
the lane curves out of sight.
No sound of an engine, only
a downpour beating tin.

I have been afraid of this
vertigo of the heart,
vigil in inky rain,
everything swallowed up except
the dull bulk of the barn,
the outline of a hedge bank,
the black flames of trees.

Nothing can help me now.
Not even what I have known
for years and failed to tell you:
what binds this holding
to the heavens, and keeps the heavens
from flying apart forever
is the secret, even pull of the dark matter
hidden among the stars.

Keats Has a Line

(for my friend)

We roamed for hours. Along scented lanes
unravished by the bypass or the builder
we spoke of love and its attendant pains
and hopes that we forgot as we grew older.

The Cat Girl played her piano unaware
that in the cold and dark we watched and lingered
long, to admire her profile and her hair
and longed to be caressed by those fine fingers.

'Keats has a line in *Lamia*,' Martin said,
'about the summer heaven, blue and clear
between two marble shafts, seen from a bed
made sweet by use.' His words fell on my ear
richly. And rich the memory of that year
now I am old and tired and worn, and he is dead.

The Invention of the Wheel Comes of Age

(for my son)

That dashing Italian pram, *Giordano*,
rode high across Hampstead Heath
on the chrome of its undercarriage.

The superstructure, finished
in blinding white luxury plastic,
reflected the brilliance of spring.

Honeycombed in blanket
your round little features peered
from under the shell-shaped hood.

We smiled as your charcoal eyes drank
the parade of blue and treetops,
the amazing arriving world.

Our Lady of Paris

(for my daughter)

'It's a grasshopper, Notre Dame,'
my Serbian friend insisted.
'When you are there you think
flying buttresses are legs.'
In the morning sun your mother and I
sat in the little square
to the east, where the Seine divides
and the buttresses *were* legs,
while you, daisy-faced in a white sun-hat,
gazed up from your blue pushchair
at the huge thing hulking against the sky.

Twenty-eight years later
my Serbian friend is dead.
There is no-one I can complain to
that the buttresses are just buttresses,
that Notre Dame never left the Quay of Flowers
to sing in harvest fields, that its empty amour
blocks the sunset as your mother and I
sit in the little square, dwarfed as ants,
dazed as ants who lose
their eggs in a scalding flood. The past
has altered. I see it as it was, too late.
Too late even then, even though
you were so small and warm
and humorous, alive, our lady of Paris.

Henry’s Bridge

The river: slow between levees
whose grass is rubbed by soles
and rutted by cycle wheels.
The wind is a voice in power lines
(what does it say?)

A day like any other?
No, you have come unbidden
to walk. I have left my work
willingly, willingly
(set that down).

River of absent fish
surveyed by a slumped heron.
Your eyes play guessing games.
We step over lumps of iron
(smoothed by time).

Clouds like ink in water.
Grass rubbed by soles.
Bare trees in drifts, rectangular towers.
Golfers in perfect pullovers on green
(across the water).

The sun muddles through
and now: Simon's Bridge
Donated by Henry Simon.
‘Not Henry's Bridge?’ you ask
(amused by its green girders).

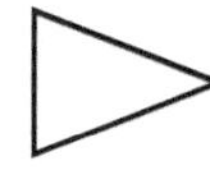

Now shall we return
along the slow river
forever disappearing
ahead into the bend?
(Many have passed this way.)

You will catch a bus? Yes,
a bus. Will it bring you back?
Will you buy a return?
The clouds are ink in water
(your hair is black).

How do places colour
the cross-threads of our work?
How do we deal with them?
How do we set them down?
('It depends,' you say.)

Goodbye, goodbye in the sun
where once a stone trough stood
mentioned in a book
stuffed with our city
(oh, what was it called?)

What could I say to you
apart from another question?
The sky was vitreous blue.
A day like any other?
(willingly, willingly).

Letters To My Daughter

1

Hawking says time, elastic
and hooked like a cycle bungee,
can suddenly snap back:

I tap the brass fox knocker.
Hello from the Asian boys
going in and out next door.

Your variegated laurel.
Your rippled glass.
Your shape blurred in the hall.

Tall I remember. Warm
embrace, that too. Face
an identikit from my album.

2

How long can this go on?
Two thousand seven hundred
and eighty-four days gone

since the last time we met.
How beautiful you were.
Forgive how little I said.

But how could you listen then,
smug, nose in the air,
party feet turned in?

Spring. The borders packed
With scents. My plan to forget
your coldness blocked.

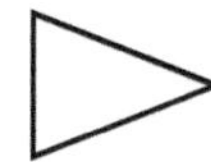

3

Shall we be meeting soon
when the white owl flies
out of the creaking barn?

Or at the bluestone gate
below Carningli where
the forest path comes out?

Will you amaze with a rustle
of dead hag's-taper stalks
the garden at Picton Castle

and when the new year chimes
argue with me there
beside the clumps of thyme?

4

A window coloured to show
a sailing ship at sunset.
Framed rules. No music, no.

Neck weals carefully hidden
by silk. Around one wrist
a colourful braid ribbon.

Smug, nose in the air.
Why do we never meet?
Or are you everywhere?

The moon is above the barn.
Smell: I'm planing wood.
Listen: the wind is calm.

Song For My Granddaughter

I'm going to hold on and on
while we no longer meet.
I'm going to live with the threat
of eternal separation.

I study your photograph.
Futile. Your features freeze.
But sometimes on the breeze
I almost hear you laugh.

Those big parabolic dishes
at Jodrell Bank, fifty yards
apart, made our whispered words
so clear! And how auspicious

that day seems when I phone
and the conversation drags
like a fire of unseasoned logs
and you'd rather be left alone.

I'm going to hold on through
the scenes of life, as in
the story of Tam Lin.
I believe, I believe in you.

The stars have disappeared
as I blunder in dark and mist
in search of the keys I lost
with a torch that seems to have died

but I know, I know they're
up there enduring patiently
till the marvellous moment they
are ready to reappear.

After You've Gone

(for my grandsons)

Once again I tidy
the toys you scrambled for when you arrived.
The two narrow beds you slept in
hard to reach across the litter of
a besieging army of tiny men. Their hands
are clips designed for holding
swords, ramrods, banners with heraldry,
laser guns. I rattle them and their materiel –
jetpacks, a green chair, a small black pig –
into the crude wooden bus I made you
out of an offcut. All aboard!
You're leaving again for Shelf Land.

Now I can get in close enough to strip
the bedding to bare duvet,
autumn shades of mattress.
The pillows are still dented where you slept
satisfied after we read you stories
of heroes old and modern. I love these signs
of your separate lives, the smell of your hair and skin.
Under the pillows two besiegers,
a knight with a helmet Dürer might draw,
a pirate captain without his plastic hair –
the favourites. Loved while you were here
they reach out with stiff arms
and empty hands designed for holding.

About the Author

Alex Barr was born in Manchester and educated at Manchester Grammar School.

After seven years in journalism in various cities, he studied at Portsmouth Polytechnic, gained a Diploma in Architecture with distinction, and worked as a senior lecturer in the School of Architecture at Manchester Metropolitan University.

On retirement he and his wife Rosemarie, a ceramic artist, moved to a smallholding in West Wales. The Pembrokeshire landscape has inspired much of his later work.

This collection includes poems which appeared in leading magazines in the UK, USA, and Canada.

❀

By the same author:

Poetry

Letting in the Carnival
Henry's Bridge
Orchards (with Peter Oram)
Alex's Little Book of Sixty Pseudo-haiku

Fiction

My Life With Eva
Take a Look at Me-e-e!

Acknowledgements

Publications in which the following poems appeared:

'Bedding Plants For My Father' in *Peterloo Poets Prize Anthology*

'Dark Matter' and 'Henry's Bridge' in *Poetry Wales*

'Our Lady of Paris' in *Apalachee Review*

'Letters To My Daughter' in *Scintilla*

'After You've Gone' in *Grain*

'Daffodil Ride' in *The Dark Horse*

'Keats Has a Line' in *The MacGuffin*

www.ingramcontent.com/pod-product-compliance
Lightning Source LLC
LaVergne TN
LVHW080206180826
845678LV00023BA/1759
* 9 7 9 8 3 6 1 2 8 2 9 7 5 *